GLOBAL 1

The Lockdown Limericks
of Agatha and Winifred

Edited by Margaret Stokes and Wendy Neale

A SHAMLOCK PRODUCTION

Copyright © 2022 Margaret Stokes and Wendy Neale.

No part of this publication may be reproduced, distributed, or transmitted in any form or by any means, including photocopying, recording, or other electronic or mechanical methods, or by any information storage and retrieval system without the prior written permission of the publisher, except in the case of very brief quotations embodied in critical reviews and certain other noncommercial uses permitted by copyright law.

ISBN: 9798355194581

Perpetrators: Margaret Stokes and Wendy Neale.

Cover design, layout, illustrations and general interference: Anton Stokes.

Margaret Stokes and Wendy Neale are the full-time, though reluctant, carers for Agatha and Winifred. It was they who suggested to them the idea of limerick writing in the somewhat vain hope that it would keep their fading wits from complete atrophy during the long days of lockdown. Mmes Stokes and Neale have had to edit out many an obscenity that the two old girls came up with. If they have missed a few, please accept their apologies.

Acknowledgements:

Special thanks to HM Government for creating the unique environment from which we all needed to break free.

Extra special thanks to Anton Stokes without whose unstinting endeavours this volume would never have seen the light of day.

Two O.A.P's who were scatty
Found lockdown was driving them batty,
So they e-mailed in rhyme,
One line at a time
And created some verse that was natty.

They challenged each other, each week
With lines that were odd and oblique,
But they always replied,
(From no subject they shied.)
We think that they might be unique.

A foolish young lad from Nantucket

Got his head wedged in a bucket.

He staggered about

'Cos he couldn't see out.

Fell flat on his face and said, "Oh dear".

Since the pandemic arrived,

Not many people have thrived.

Be it lock-down or lock-up

It's felt like a cock up.

But I'm glad that, so far, I've survived.

A scary young lady from Surrey

Caused all of her neighbours to worry.

On Halloween night

She gave them a fright

When her hands and her face grew all furry.

That same lovely lady from Surrey

Had to get home in a hurry.

Her options were few.

She needed the loo

(She should never have eaten that curry.)

A chap, whom I knew was a Swede,

Told me, whenever he weed,

He climbed up a mountain

And sent out a fountain,

Fulfilling some long standing need.

There was a young lady from Dorset

Who got herself trapped in her corset.

She tried to escape,

Got pulled out of shape:

That's what ensues if you force it.

A very fast lass from Kilkenny,

Whose lovers were varied and many,

Gave all that she had

To the good and the bad

And never charged them a penny.

A grumpy old feller from Fife

Lost all of his kids and his wife.

It was not unexpected

For when he reflected,

He'd not cracked a smile in his life.

An eccentric old lady from Leeds,

Ran around town planting seeds.

But what made it odd

Was the silly old sod

Was only distributing weeds.

A vain little madam called Anna,

Studied her face through a scanner.

But it gave her a scare

And she started to swear

In a most unladylike manner.

I'm a wee bit concerned for my friend

Who spends all her time in Southend,

Where she juggles live eels

Just to see how it feels.

I fear she's a tad round the bend.

There was a young woman called Tracy,

A little bit, what I'd call, racy.

Her top was well stacked

But her bottom quite lacked

Any size, and her knickers were lacy.

On bonfire night, with a rocket

Carelessly shoved in his pocket

A young boy took flight.

T'was a wondrous sight.

(If you've never tried it, don't knock it!)

My friend had a very tame rabbit

Who displayed a peculiar habit.

If he spotted a dick

His reactions were quick

And he'd suddenly jump up and grab it.

I have an OLD friend, name of Wendy

Whose wardrobe is frightfully trendy.

On top of all that,

She's not gone to fat

So she's really attractive… and bendy.

A guy who was quite microscopic

Spent his whole life in the tropics.

When queried by all,

"Why are you so small ?"

He said, "Maybe it's you that's myopic!"

A telesales guy from New Delhi

Could never quite tell just how well he

Would fare as a father

So, in rather a lather,

The thought turned his legs into jelly.

To determine the speed of light,

I set off on a hazardous flight,

But I hit a live wire

And my ass caught on fire

Just South of the Isle of Wight.

There was an old chap from New York

Who sat down, quite hard, on a fork.

Paralysed by the shock,

He called for the doc

Who bunged up the wound with a cork.

A handsome young fellow named Michael

Said, "I think that having a bike'll

Make life much easier

Though possibly queasier

'Cos I always feel sick when I cycle."

A well brought-up fellow called David

Was polite and quite well behavéd

But his dog scared the town

And was caught and put down

'Cos the vet said, "He's mangy and rabid."

On the wonderful planet of Zyte

The sun comes up twice every night.

Though you might think this wrong,

The beings on Fong

Have the same, and think it quite right.

There was a young man from Glamorgan

Who was very adept on his organ.

He played it so well

It caused quite a swell;

The resulting conclusion was foregone.

A Brit who got lost in Madrid.

(Oh no, not Madrid, God forbid!)

Found his satnav was duff;

Well you can't trust that stuff,

And a map would cost less than ten quid.

There was a young lass from Hyde Park

Who would do anything for a lark.

With a flick of her wrist

She'd uncover her cyst

Which mostly she kept in the dark.

A super-intelligent goat

Decided to take the first boat

Round the Islands of Greece,

Where he found inner peace

And took a few moments to gloat.

Jamie Wong, who lived in Hong Kong

Always thought that his legs were too long,

But in spite of his pleas,

There were no guarantees

That shortening them wouldn't go wrong.

A nun who had mislaid her wimple

Was dismayed that her prominent pimple

Would now be in sight

And that it just might

Detract from the charm of her dimple.

A man with no name, just a number,

Who sailed on a giant cucumber,

In search of his roots

With a cargo of fruits,

Ran aground near the mouth of the Humber.

A Reverend Mother named Celia

Was sorting through memorabilia

When something went pop

And she came to a stop

And thought she should check her camellia.

A young curate from Havant, in Hants

Led a life quite devoid of romance

But he fancied the vicar

Who was older and slicker

And he thought he could teach her to dance.

A cyclist who suffered from piles

Was well known for his cunning wiles

So, in spite of the pain

And the freezing cold rain,

Used ointment, and went on for miles.

A bright young fellow called Newton

Had to have bread without gluten,

So he sat 'neath his tree

Scoffing quinoa for tea

With jam, on a comfortable futon.

A fantastically fit lass called Margaret

Said, "I wonder exactly how far I'd get

If I walked twenty miles

Over fields, jumping stiles?

Well anyway, that's my new targaret."

A French lorry driver in Kent

Regretted that he ever went

To deliver to Brits.

The ungrateful shits

Left him to linger till Lent.

I knew an unhappy old trucker

Who put on his best bib and tucker

Which had seen better days

From a happier phase

When his truck was not stuck without succour.

A newly-accredited witch

Crash landed her broom in a ditch,

Which would have been fine,

But she'd been on the wine

So was forced to relinquish her pitch.

A paralytic old drunk

Woke up with a mouth like a skunk.

He said, "Gawd, I think

That maybe I stink,

But I'm still a handsome great hunk."

A young chap with a very small dick,

(Both short and not very thick)

Took some special blue pills

That made him grow gills,

So he dived in the pond, and was sick.

A guy who was missing an ear

Thought he had nothing to fear,

But folks can be mean,

And will soon vent their spleen

If they think the poor bugger can't hear.

In Egypt, a lesser known mummy

Was unravelled with food in his tummy.

As the sight made me heave,

It was hard to believe

That someone had once found that yummy.

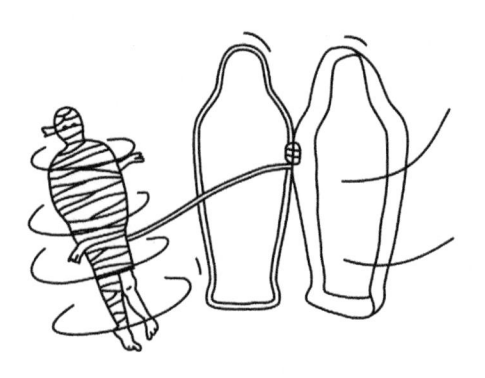

A visiting chap at Niagara,

By mistake, took a dose of viagra.

The resultant outpouring

Matched the cataract's roaring,

And someone yelled, "Abracadabra!"

A dropout who lived by the ocean

Was a gentle soul, full of emotion,

But he had a dark past,

It's effect on him vast.

It wasn't the life he'd have chosen.

A wee lad from The Emerald Isle

Had not seen his Dad for a while,

Or his Mum, for that matter,

(Who was mad as a hatter)

So he moved himself up to Argyle.

A fellow I know, name of Stephen,

Had teeth that were crossed and uneven.

When he got to the dentist

(A Seventh Day Adventist)

He'd something that he could believe in.

I was playing a nice game of chess,

Not a game I know well, I confess,

When it suddenly clicked

And I knew if I picked

Up a penguin, I'd get in a mess.

A chap near the South coast of Spain

Was waiting for forecasts of rain.

When none were forthcoming,

He checked his own plumbing

And went out and pissed on the plain.

I've had my first dose of the vaccine,

And had to admire the slick routine.

There was one little prick,

Which I hope did the trick.

But he looked like a bit of a has-been.

A lad from the Isle of Capri

Climbed to the top of a tree.

He wasn't sure why,

But he felt he could fly

And he landed inside A and E.

Colleen from The Emerald Isle

Was spiteful and really quite vile.

She tied children to trees.

Oh what a great wheeze.

Their predicament caused her to smile.

There was a young lass called Octavia

Who had a fine house in Belgravia

But her habit of spending

Was just never ending,

So she's now had to move to Moldavia.

A young lass who lived on the hill

Was more of a Jack than a Jill.

Her mother once said

She was wrong in the head

In choosing a gal for her thrill.

A drunken old sot from Kilbride

Climbed to the top of a slide

Already cross eyed

And with legs spread out wide,

He yelled as he fell, "What a ride!"

There was a young fellow from Spain.

Who was at it again and again.

When they said he must stop it,

He told them to drop it,

So they did, and it caused him great pain.

A merchant who hailed from Kashmir

Was a dealer in high octane beer.

The stuff was so strong

That before very long

Its effects on the brain were severe.

A gal with a face like a horse

Had a husband who showed no remorse

When he took her to Aintree

And said, smiling faintly,

"I thought you should go on a course."

A handsome young lad from Gibraltar

Had a mule that would constantly falter.

On his way to get married,

The wretched thing tarried

And made him too late at the altar.

A lass with a lisp, from Alaska

Moved herself down to Nebraska.

Seems so silly to say

Why she went off that day.

I don't really know, so I'll ask her.

A fellow who loved to play cricket

Suffered a wound at the wicket.

With a scab, newly grown,

Folks said, "Leave it alone.

It'll never heal up if you pick it."

An old friend of mine, name of Aggie

No longer has clothes that are baggy.

With her needles and pins,

She disguises her sins,

Which by now are many and saggy.

A crowd on the banks of the Nile

Were intrigued by the large crocodile

That loitered nearby

With a tear in his eye

And planned how to seize them, by guile.

A new young arrival in China

Had just disembarked from a liner

When she suddenly thought,

I'm glad that I brought

That cream for my itchy vagina.

A rancher who lived way out West
Considered himself quite the best
As he rode on his land,
With his infamous band,
In just chaps and a dirty old vest.

A chap with erectile disfunction

Said, "I once had a dick like a truncheon."

But his wife said, "My dear,

I have made it quite clear

We do not discuss this over luncheon."

There once was a coven of witches

Who were plagued by a series of glitches.

Every spell they attempted

Went wrong, none exempted,

And they all doubled over in stitches.

I thought of becoming a nun,

But then I'd miss out on the fun.

What I hadn't foreseen,

At the age of sixteen

Was, of fun, there would be almost none.

A skier set off on the slopes;

(No knowledge but very high hopes.)

She crashed into a fence

And in her defence

Said, "Nobody showed me the ropes."

I met a most amorous frog

Who'd been hiding under a log

Not sure if to kiss it

But silly to miss it,

So we kissed, and I've now got a sprog.

A couple who lived in Bridgend

Drove each other clean round the bend.

From morning till night

They did nothing but fight,

And she finished him off in the end.

A silly young woman called Maisie

Painted her face like a daisy.

When asked what she'd done,

She said, "It was such fun."

So all her friends said she was crazy.

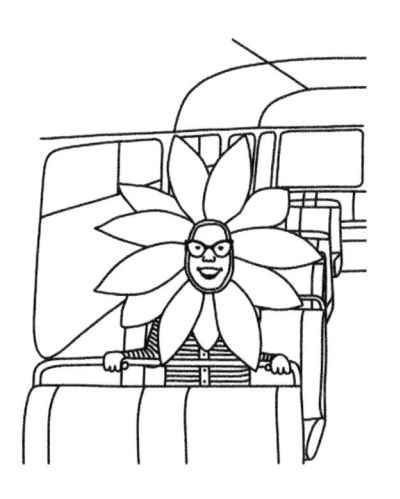

When asked if he'd play Widow Twankey,

An actor became rather cranky.

"But I'm due to play Lear

At the end of the year"

He replied, in a tone somewhat swanky.

A poet whose thoughts came in rhyme,

Seemed to spend most of his time

Getting them written down

Seeking out great renown:

But his wife said his rhymes were a crime.

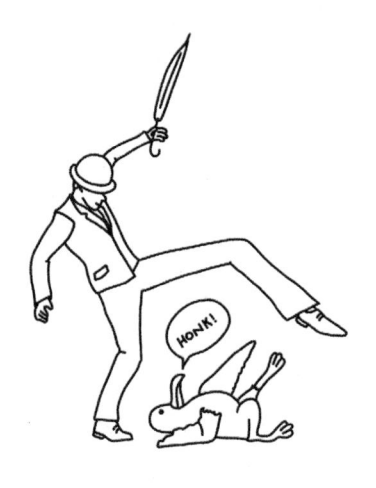

A fellow who lived near Kings Cross

Found a very lame albatross

Who'd dropped from the sky

With a terrible cry,

But the bastard did not give a toss.

I was sitting here thinking of dinner,

And if Chinese food makes you thinner.

Well, I'll walk to the shop,

And it's quite a fair hop,

So I reckon it does. It's a winner.

A Bollywood star from Mumbai

Was alarmed by a rather large fly

Which buzzed round the set

And caused her to get

Her well rehearsed lines all awry.

A chap who had just got engaged

Said, "I suddenly feel I've been caged.

Although she's a stunner,

I might do a runner

And hope that she's not too outraged."

A lady-boy out in Bangkok

Thought it was high time to shock

So he opened his dress

Which was bold, I confess,

But his member was wrapped in a sock.

A chap who was running a choir

Thought that rehearsals were dire,

But his charm and his wit

Pulled them out of the shit,

And the concert saw them on fire.

A pervy old Scot named Mctavity

Had sunk to the depths of depravity.

He scared girls to bits,

Made a grab for their tits,

And claimed he was just testing gravity.

My uncle who lived in Belgrade

Spent all of his life in the shade,

Which we thought was so sad,

But it wasn't as bad

As the tax bill he sought to evade.

There was a young dragon called Bill

Who developed a very bad chill,

So he couldn't breathe fire

Which for dragons, is dire.

He just had to hide and keep still.

A big lad who came from Cape Cod

Worked every day with a hod,

Moving bricks shoulder high

In a constant supply.

But now he's bent double, poor sod.

A rich farming man from Marseilles

Did all of his work in a day;

So he drove to his yacht,

Which he did quite a lot.

It was where he made most of his hay.

Poor James craved the life of a monk,

A waste because he was a hunk,

But his calling was strong

And he knew all along

That girls sent him into a funk.

A Teddy bear sitting alone,

In a run-down pedestrian zone,

Watched the people pass by

With a tear in his eye

As he wanted a home of his own.

A young man who crewed on a yacht

Thought one of his shipmates was hot.

His approaches were crass.

When he fondled her ass,

He went over the side, like a shot.

A winger who played for West Ham

Ate nothing but onions and spam,

But the fall-out from that

Sometimes blew off his hat,

And caused his opponents to scram.

A chap from the island of Crete

Had issues with both of his feet.

It was not just the smell;

They were swollen, as well:

A feature brought on by the heat.

What shall we do with Mathilda?

Someone just told me she killed a

Snake in the grass

Who had bitten her ass

And the sight of it, dead, simply thrilled her.

A cat who was out on the prowl

Was after a rather large owl,

But the owl was quicker:

His talons were thicker,

So puss just bailed out with a howl.

I once took a trip to Helsinki

With a friend, but I really don't think he

Ever wants to go back.

There's a terrible lack

Of the things that he likes, which are kinky.

I'm writing a letter to Santa

To ask for a big elephant, a

Real huge one of course,

Though it could be a horse;

And please tell me Rudolph can canter.

I really love Christmas dinner.

Every flavour a winner.

I will just scoff the lot

While it's still piping hot,

Then wonder why I'm not thinner.

A bloke who had suffered for years

As the butt of the joke for his peers,

Won a lottery prize

That would water your eyes,

And they turned up in droves to say, "Cheers!"

I'm never averse to a verse:

My preoccupation gets worse!

With a pen in my hand,

My horizons expand,

One rhyme at a time, it's a curse.

For Christmas I really want duck

I could catch a wild one, with luck:

Then I'd have to pluck it,

So let's just say f**k it.

The very idea seems to suck.

My dear little cousin in Wales

Would always queue up for the sales.

She'd get everything cheap,

And she once bought a sheep

But she lost it again, in the vales.

Our dear old puss cat, a tabby,

Is toothless and just a bit shabby.

We feed her minced fish

In her own special dish

But she's downright ungrateful-and crabby.

I wandered the streets of Cologne

And wondered why I was alone,

Then thought back to my past,

Which had passed far too fast,

And all of the chances I'd blown.

A hapless old man from Hong Kong

Noticed a terrible pong,

Then he took a quick glance

At the seat of his pants,

And realised something was wrong.

In England, along the South coast

If you look hard enough, there's a most

Awful caravan park

Which glows bright in the dark.

In lumens, it's quite overdosed.

It seems, once again, Easter's here.

It comes, as we know, every year,

But they change when it is,

Which puts me in a tizz.

Has it come? Has it gone? Is it near?

It was Saturday night in the hall;

Just a small local hop, not a ball,

But it snowed hard at seven,

And by half past eleven

They were tucked up in bed, one and all.

Some people who live overseas

Make any beasts' milk into cheese;

From a goat, mare or ewe,

And that's only a few,

And even from yaks, if you please!

We 'ad us a picnic in t'park,

And stayed out till it were quite dark.

But on us way back

We strayed off t' track,

And got us home just afore t'lark.

The dentist was always quite willing

To do an emergency filling

But a patient, still numb,

Once bit off his thumb

In shock, at the sight of his billing.

A gal who was raised on a farm

Combined wit and wisdom with charm,

Which she used every day

To get her own way,

But she never caused anyone harm.

A big guy got stuck in a chair

And sank to the depths of despair,

'Cos when people passed by

They took shots, on the sly,

And posted for others to share.

A charming young fellow named Steve

Had several tricks up his sleeve.

He could conjure up mice

And doves, at a price,

And stuff that you wouldn't believe.

I'd just started crossing the road,

And spotted a very wide load

That was parked on the bend,

And could not comprehend

Why the eejit had stopped for a toad.

I'm struggling to find the right rhyme

And really don't have that much time,

'Cos it's time for some food

And I know it's quite crude

But abandoning would be a crime.

Did you ever hear about Charlie

Who used to roar round on a Harley?

The noise that he made

Was so bad, I'm afraid,

That it made all the neighbours quite snarly.

I once took a trip to Bengal

Where Calcutta had held me in thrall

Till I found out, too late,

That the tigers I hate,

Lived only just over the wall.

I encountered a bear with one ear

And wondered how much he could hear.

He could certainly see

And came charging at me.

Serves me right for getting so near.

A guy who was from Albuquerque,

Had a past that was known to be murky,

But he never replied

When anyone cried,

"We know what you did with a turkey!"

A man who lived in Winchester,

Who became a real shrewd investor,

Bought houses to let,

From the gains of a bet,

And owned a whole district of Leicester.

I saw something strange in the wood.

I'd show it to you if I could,

But I've never been back

'Cos I can't find the track

Or the actual place where it stood.

I once tried to fly, though I shouldn't,

When everyone told me I wouldn't,

In a Reliant Robin,

All cylinders throbbin',

With the wings blue-tacked on; and I couldn't.

Our rhyming must come to an end

Before we both go round the bend,

But one thing's so true:

It's much better with two,

And verse is more fun with a friend.

We've run out of rhymes for a while.

Some of our subjects were vile

But whatever ensued,

Be it proper or rude,

We hope that they brought you a smile.

Now it's your turn:

The first of your 5-a-day

For mental health

To keep boredom at bay:

There was a young man from Caerphilly

....

....

....

....

Printed in Great Britain
by Amazon